Holding Ground

poems by Tanis MacDonald

holding
ground

poems by Tanis MacDonald

SERAPHIM EDITIONS

The publisher gratefully acknowledges the financial assistance
of the Canada Council.

Published in 2000 by
Seraphim Editions
970 Queen Street East
P.O. Box 98174
Toronto, Ontario
Canada M4M 1J0

Canadian Cataloguing in Publication Data

MacDonald, Tanis, 1962–
    Holding ground

Poems.
ISBN 0-9699639-6-3

    I. Title.

PS8575.D6657H65 2000   C811'.54   C00-900400-9
PR9199.3.M33H65 2000

Design: Sue Meggs-Becker
Cover Photo: Tom Lackey

Printed and bound in Canada by Métrolitho

For my parents: terra firma

Contents

Part I

A Blur of Green

Given

I WAS A summer vacation

> a cottage-country party
>> a Lake-of-the-Woods   pine-filled   mosquito night
>> a midnight dance under a July moon

> with the tall boy from Sault Sainte Marie
>> so blond his hair cooled my mother's eyes
>> his long Norwegian bones lifted her
>> in a waltz she thought she'd never dance

> free of her parents' divorce   her solid body
>> chestnut hair searching for the moment
>> the hot shame of it did not burn her
>> here at her aunt's cottage where no one
>> knew her out under the band shell stars

> in the woods walking home
>> they spread a cool balm on their foreheads
>>> breathed each other awake
>>> gathered my sound within

> between them I sang
> a thread of notes   a string of words

> long months she was sent to sit with her mistake   her
> fevered body pulsing with me   her naked fingers
> shrieking   but I spoke in her secret ear

mother listen I will be born listen I will be mother I am
coming I am yours get ready mother I am your first
flower root me deep be prepared mother

and she
    and she

        took a thousand shallow breaths
        and gave me away to the world,
        crying

this hot coal
this speaking plant
this naked voice

                is not mine

Nobody's Girl

AFTER *Oh Canada,*
>   we stand to the left of our desks
>   heads bowed, eyes closed for the Lord's Prayer,
>   but somewhere around *forgive us our trespasses*
>   a small mouth worships my right cheek,
>   and I open my eyes
>   too surprised to pray
>   after a kiss.

He watches me across the aisle,
striped shirt and straight dark bangs
and I don't move – a weary bird
settles inside me,
ruffles its feathers to sleep

but then another girl laughs
and his pointy boy ears pink at the tips,
his knees buckle.

He cries
because at eight, love is already
sad, a small scandal.
His kiss lies on my skin
like a cloud,
marks me nobody's girl
before the class mumbles
amen.

Eating Crow

an old family recipe

SELECT A BIG crow.
      These birds are rarely plump and juicy,
      but their bodies thicken somewhat for winter.
      A Northern bird harvested by hand
      in early fall is best
      and will fill you
      without the distraction of flavour.

      Roll out pastry.
      Do not worry about flakiness or lumps.
      This is a container for crow only.

      Next, prepare bird.
      Pluck, or for deep contrition,
      simply wrap bird in pastry.
      Do not de-beak.
      Feet should poke up through the crust.
      Bake in a shallow pan
      at 350 degrees for forty minutes,
      or until talons droop.

      Remove from oven barehanded;
      leave burns undressed and eat
      in the immediate presence of your betters.

      Smile as you chew,
      but don't let the feathers show
      between your teeth.

The Onion Eater

THE CHILD BITES into
    the pungent globe
    as though it was an apple,
    the scrape of her small teeth
    reveals the layers beneath.

    The onion bursts to juice
    like any fruit, a peach
    or an orange, and she sucks
    the sharp nectar, crunches
    the bulb to bits that cling
    to her pink gums, extra
    teeth when she grins.

    She never does this at home,
    this trick that burns her lips
    and riots on her tongue, only in this house,
    where the ginger cat lies on the table,
    Cleopatra among the ketchup and relish,
    and before it is shooed off,
    everyone laughs

when she lifts a clean white slice
between thumb and forefinger,
delicate as a stinging doily,
and bites down, her eyes
sprung with acid tears,

and she asks, politely
as she can with a mouth full of bees,
could I have a whole onion
all to myself please

South of Discovery

Far north.
    The windy river
    stretched away
    to long ice,
    and Franklin, bulky
    in Royal Navy blue
    and square-toed boots commanded
    three officers, eighteen voyageurs
    and one servant
    further north to the sun.

    Past caribou crossings
    gunpowder cracked the air,
    pale hands scratched
    paper that water
    would turn to
    salted mush.

    Most ate their boots,
    a last meal by Starvation Bay,
    but Franklin lived,
    was knighted in uniform,
    gold braid dangling
    from epaulettes like moss,

had a school named after him
on Corydon Avenue in Winnipeg,
a flat grey building
stuffed with grades one to six,
softball uniforms green and white,
SJF in silver on the sleeves.

On any spring evening, silver
glints in the long light like the lens
of a spyglass. A runner rounds third
for home, legs a blur of green against
the brown grass, a last tall tree
against the tundra.

Lidded

IN THE PHOTO my cowboy hat lids me keeps my head on
keeps my thoughts in   safe in the backyard my father's
hat rides high on his forehead a joke borrowed for the
camera   mine is a serious weight stores dreams until they
ripen mats down my hair a white straw passport to the
roaring world   neighbours see me bob by the window
the snap brim the cloth plume and know I am The Hat

my head grows I buy a bigger hat   the whole city is
hazed with burning sugar beets   people cough and choke
but safe under my hat I'm out on the bald prairie riding a
big bay into the west the sun burning hot dust but my hat
cools me   no smoke no squint no sunburn I ride forever
past scrub and gopher holes

Falcon Lake

ALONE, MY BROTHER fishes,
     perched on the stern's gunwale,
     tipping the canoe's bow up
     to drip steady as a tap
     back into the lake, a slice of red
     on blue, a floating smile.

From the shore, our father
calls. My brother turns
too quickly, arcs back.
The lake covers him without
a sound, but the bow slaps down
like a beaver tail,
his fishing rod
twangs off-key

until he splutters to the surface,
flips a spume of water
from his hair, surprised to hear
trees shout his name,
shocked to find himself
swallowed.

Social Studies

His RIGHT EYE was blue glass
    but caught every spitball-
    flicking boy

    in social studies class,
    he gave us walking lessons

    "A Man," he said
    and nostrils flared,
    shoulders broadened,
    he strode across the room,
    a warrior
    a king

    "A Woman," and
    he floated by, hips swaying
    like palm frond fans

    he clenched a smile like
    a stogie between his big teeth,
    and we stumbled up
    from our desks
    on toothpick legs,
    his single blue eye
    still as a window
    framing the flat world
    beyond

Five Foot Positions

ALL THOSE MORNINGS I stood in a black
    leotard and tights with holes cut
    at toe and heel, my feet bare or sheathed
    in pink leather all those mornings

    I rested my hand atop the springy balsam
    of the ballet barre, breathed through my back
    and pulled up, pulled up, braced for
    the swift hard prod

    the ballet master's bony finger poked ribs
    and gouged hipbones, bored a hole
    in the centre of my back, a spot that never
    healed, the small wound of a bad dancer

    his jab made me jump and him scowl every time,
    all those mornings I *plie'd* and pointed,
    ignored the sour ache of my calves, never *jete'd*
    high enough but practiced all five foot positions

    in my sleep, woke up with cramps some nights
    from turning my feet out at the hips. I was never good.
    Those mornings when traffic honked and the piano
    played the same twenty bars of music over and over

    I watched the black spandex back in front of me
    and tried to bend without breaking.

Bread and Salt

HER LEGS SWOLLEN to tree trunks beneath her house
dress, she shuffles from stove to formica table and back,
heaping chewable treasures high – a starchy Tower of
Babel – but the spiked Cyrillic alphabet silences me
(*kutia, kalach, babka* ...).

My boyfriend is upstairs doing whatever nineteen-year-
old boys do when they leave their girlfriends trapped
with Ukrainian mothers.

In her humid kitchen, my sedate heritage covers me like
a tarp. I can't see through to her, plying me with
nourishment an hour after dinner. I am not negotiating
this summit well. She can't understand why I'm not
hungry, why I'm not eating her food, why she shouldn't
go to such trouble for me, just me.

She knows enough English to keep people away, but not
enough to lure me into her cabbaged domain, smiling
our mutual muteness as plates and casserole dishes pile
up, more ammunition in our war of food, but it's a
stand-off, I'm not eating, she must get the message, I
can't possibly consume this much, she can't possibly
expect me to, but she does.

The table legs shudder beneath a stack of steaming crockery. She draws up a chair, sits, folds perogie-chapped hands in her prim aproned lap, utters one accented motherword, eat. Smiles.

Her smile. A cold journey to Canada, daughters rattling at her in English, silent sons twice her size, bringing home skinny blond girls who can't cook, don't even eat (*this one here is a stick! – she needs koubasa – lots of it*).

My sleeves roll up, my belt loosens.

She smiles.

Service with a Smile

AMONG THE CRASH and clatter of dishes,
    always a spot of gravy on my white cuff,
    displeasing the green eye-shadowed
    new deli manager who didn't know
    how to speed order pick-up,
    couldn't tell a good pickle from bad,
    couldn't even find the words to tell me
    my earrings were too big, blossoming
    blue sparklers. During the dinner shift
    I carried corned beef and cabbage
    to a ten-table section while she struggled
    to choose the proper managerial phrase
    and I loaded plates up my arm and
    pretended I had no idea what
    the problem was.

    At midnight, foot-swollen and bone-sore,
    my back sang a scale of grinding cracks
    as I sat in the corner booth and emptied
    my apron of sour money and filmy credit slips.
    I smelled of mustard even on my days off,
    and my boyfriend lost his head one night
    and heaved a whole tray of glasses at
    the Portuguese grill cook, fifteen transparent
    missiles exploded on the grill, showered
    slivers on the cook's curled back,
    but the cook was a decent guy
    and never took it out on me,
    my orders up fresh and hot,
    every time.

Cowgirl

ONE SUMMER I waited tables in a country-and-western
bar and wore a cowgirl uniform that was so cheesy all I
could do was make it look like a choice. Bought a cheap
hip holster and two plastic six-shooters, strapped on
spurs that did not jingle jangle jingle but rattled like a
tubercular sidewinder when I walked over to say *what
can I get you?*

All the other girls were scared of cows and their
boyfriends went to Queens or Laurier and picked them
up after shift, but I knew the smell of cowshit from
shovelling it and my boyfriend had just ridden off into
the sunset without so much as a thank you ma'am.

I wore out my smile, I wore out miles of boot leather
from bar to patio, I bore out too many John Wayne
drawls from guys who said *little lady, you look like a
straight shooter,* but one night a drunk shoved his hand
up my skirt, and I dropped my tray and pulled my gun,
smacked the plastic barrel between his eyes and he
dropped into a chair like I had shot him and I hated the
moment when I had to make a joke of it, blew fake
smoke from the gun and holstered it to all the laughs
from the big-bellied guys who tipped me twenty cents a
round.

The bouncer was called Abel, *that's Mr. Abel to you*, dark
as midnight chocolate and ten times as bad for you. He
wore the biggest Stetson in the bar, his bulk hovered at
the edge of my section, calm as ice on a scraped knee.
Once a table of frat boys wouldn't pay, saying *what time
do you get off,* and suddenly Abel's arm was light as a flag
around my shoulder and he smiled and said *how's my
woman treatin' you boys* and when I looked again, the
table was a flutter of bills. Abel said I could call him by
his first name as long as I told no one what it was.

I stuffed my tips in a mason jar. I threw away the plastic
guns. I kept Abel's given name a secret.

Wash Day

I NEVER BELIEVED
    work was worship
    until the fat woman
    at the laundromat
    scooped hot armfuls
    of cotton from the dryer's
    tumble, folded faded t-shirts
    as if it mattered
    where each crease fell,
    placed an oatmeal cookie
    on the grubby palm
    of a blank-faced boy,
    while soap blossomed
    in the round washer
    windows and winter
    mud splayed the floor.
    She placed her fleshy palm
    in the centre of the child's
    red-ravelling back,
    propelling him and his cookie
    back to his mother
    with a nudge and a belief
    in clean clothes
    for tomorrow's
    eight-day
    week.

In the Back Garden

RHUBARB GREW WILD and lush like a weed –
    stewed soft, the thick pink stalks
    boiled down to tart strings
    or dripped from a sack into jam.

I ate rhubarb pie for granted
because it was there, until
I left home and it took me years
to miss the tall fluted stalks,
the notched and nodding elephant-ear leaves.

But now a craving for rhubarb
rules my palate. I hunt it down
in markets with a loaded wallet,
bear it home strapped to the roof of my car,
green ears waving down the highway,
long stalks placid and resigned,
yielding under the knife,
oozing compliant into pies,
not cut with berries or apple,
no sweet easy tastes to smooth the way,
but straight, uncorrupted, cooked down from

the raw bite of sour stalk,
the twist and fibrous crunch,
the cry and call of wild rhubarb.

How Girls See Boys

THE EYES, THE jaw, the long muscles of his legs, beauty so blinding I always came away with optic afterburn, sunspots on my irises. I went to class just for the sight of him, listened for hours just for the moment when he would frown and ask a question

I watched for a chance to sidle up to him with an offhand remark that I'd planned for hours, wearing my blue sweater as a talisman so often he must have thought I owned no other clothes

He leaned in to kiss me under the porch light where luna moths banged against the bare bulb and my parents slept under their quilt not twenty feet away, he smiled just as our lips met, his teeth felt like pearls or stones worn smooth by the rub of saltwater, beach stones I longed to hold on my tongue but didn't, or did, but was never caught

Part II

FREESTONE

Lake Midnight

WATER REFLECTS THE stars:
   the skin of the lake
   sleek as anthracite,
   an obsidian mirror.
   Each star a planet,
   each blackness an eternity
   in the lake below.

   Cold galaxies spin
   above and beneath us,
   prone here on the pine dock,
   pinned to the purple earth.

Fragile

THE GUARDS AT the gallery
   don't want us to touch
   the art

   an outstretched arm
   or splayed fingers
   draw glares

   though the mounds
   of a Henry Moore invite
   flesh against stone

   the uniforms
   stare censures   but
   our marauding hands reach

   for air or each other
   I am told
   without a smile

   what I carry is too big
   for the gallery
   remove it or be denied

   I will not touch
   the oils or smooth stone
   this rule not made

   to be broken
   but to re-define
   what is fragile   I stroll

my small mind past
the woman with the huge proper
hat and bare breasts

I clasp my right hand behind me
a restraint to remind me
of what is touchable

                    and what is not

How Little I Know

TONIGHT IS NOT the time to confess
>how you slide into my mind when I wake
>at false dawn, even the birds fooled into song,
>questions in their throats.
>You taught me at that hour
>getting up to go home was
>a killing sort of pleasure.

>That year we wouldn't admit we were
>lovers gives me no rights at all
>but I know this: tonight the clouds
>have washed the sky opaque and ruined
>our chances of comet-watching.
>Tonight you brought me coffee in a glass,
>forgot I took no sugar. You couldn't know
>my first boyfriend used to make me coffee
>in a glass in his mother's cold kitchen
>at midnight, the two of us up late after
>kissing so much the insides of our mouths
>were swollen and we had to quit
>and talk. Tonight you are old.
>For the first time I feel the years
>hook heavy into the lapels of my coat,
>and drag me down.

>When I stand, my boots boost me taller,
>my mouth level exactly with your ear.
>I lean in, my lips close to that
>curve of flesh and cartilage, intricate as
>a jigsaw. How little I know, and how
>little a word or a kiss means to you now.

Freestone

"YOU BRUISE LIKE a peach,"
    he said.

    Purple and sick yellow
    blossomed high on my thigh.

    A peach,
    the blush of flesh
    truer than a gaze,
    textured soft but blood-red at the core,
    toxic cyanide sleeping in the heart.

    He is nine years gone.

    He never hit me,
    rarely raised his voice in anger,
    but now whenever
    my hip bumps against sharp corners,
    or elbows jab at parties,
    and I undress at night,
    I think of him and see the wound flowering,
    a slow explosion beneath my skin.

    You bruise like a peach.

Air Mail

ANOTHER HAUNTED SEASON: squash
    ripens atop my fridge,
    why don't you write? I have
    measured our cooling ground,
    meditated over stones,
    woken before the cat to feel you
    fade, no arms, no moon.

    Still the mail arrives on time,
    slaps onto the carpet at 10:15
    each morning – I hear it
    no matter where I am in the house –
    from the attic, it sounds like
    the push of flesh on flesh.

    Bills and flyers.
    I wonder if no news is good.
    Only distance can wring
    hope from the smallest omen,
    a bridge railing to lean against
    or stand atop, the current
    a road moving beneath.

    A small brown dog sleeps
    tail over nose at the foot of our bed,
    where the rose quilt my aunt sewed
    covers all that was between the lines
    you never wrote.

National Game

THE DEAF BOY from down the street
  sits with me on his way to hockey
  practice. No boy, really, a deaf man,
  with a day's beard and big hands,
  but his too-loud voice shapes sounds
  only young boys make, hooted diphthongs,
  mangled vowels. Other bus riders shoot him
  hard looks, then return to their books or
  blank reflections. *What position?*
  I ask, his eyes on my lips. If he was blind too,
  he'd touch his fingers to my lips and read me.
  What position? My brother played defense, broke
  his nose twice in a single season while I stomped
  by the echoing boards, and saw blood
  drip over the red line. The boy, the man,
  taps his cracked front tooth,
  points out a puckered weal beneath
  his eye where he caught a skate blade in a fight.
  He plays a high-scoring centre, has the wounds
  to prove it. He moans, *'ough game,*
  'ough game, shaking his shaggy head,
  his smirk a snaggle-toothed blue-jawed
  slap-shot.

Mid-March

ALL WINTER I'VE waited
    for this moment when I did not
    think of you. All winter,
    cold beneath the radiator's blocked pipes,
    you crept into each small tragedy,
    your taste for making me sweat
    stronger than morning
    coffee or malt whiskey.

You breathe too near my brain,
crowd out logic and formula, reduce
Pythagoras' theory to a squeak,
your hand flung over my hip
when I sleep, too fitful beside
your casual grip.

This spring I thought to shake off
these dead flakes of skin,
your protection too much
like pain. I admit at first I
liked it, the way I liked the first snow
gracing my window, but it kept me shut
in the house stirring lentil soup, re-reading
old letters.

Now last year's leaves stutter across my porch
and the bed is empty.

Holding Ground

SNARLED IN OUR deep roots, tangled in the dark,
  thin concentric circles tally our age in grief,
  one ring for each sorrow; we grow skin like bark,
  we forget our ache until it sprouts fresh leaf.

  In our deep roots, in those dark airless spaces
  we store pain in tight twists and do not forget
  the worst moments: they live, slow poison spreading
  beneath our soil – single shriek, the taste of dirt,

  slow-motion skid, shattering glass, snapping bone,
  each fine horror burnished by time, seasoned –
  a sliver of memory twigs us to regret, we atone
  before we grasp the low-hanging branch of reason;

  so when he dies, or she leaves, or our children take
  guns to their heads, we live through the moment, then
  we can't believe we're talking, not screaming, awake,
  not falling deep as our roots to break an axe on them,

  haul up the stubborn stump of recall, rope it to a winch
  and wrench it from the ground, pulverize the will
  that keeps us jittering this awful shuffle and clinch
  when all we ever want is to be still.

Heart Trouble

THE COLD HAND of the lake wraps around me,
     a torturer who reaches between my ribs
     to squeeze my heart,

     while submerged trees reach spiky fingers
     for my feet. Warning: *Do not*
     go beneath.

     You swim to the dock, climb out to dive,
     and I see your wet head sleek
     as a otter's, I see

     the tall pines ringing the lake, the dark sky
     on water, the way you bounce on your toes
     before you dive, and I know

     I will have heart trouble. I will return
     to the city, blurred into arrhythmia
     by my own words.

     This bitter northern bay tells our future:
     when you are gone, dissolved
     into the coming years,

     I will still have this evening,
     the water that encloses us like a quiet room,
     a heart that opens and shuts like a breathing eye.

Follow

THE PHONE CALL said you were ready to go.

    Distance throws dust in your eye,
    clouds the fox you half-tamed
    the summer you were ten, how she
    bolted in an auburn blur, glanced back
    to see you follow, then disappeared into
    a wheat field's brittle golden ocean,

    but an orange flag marked the way,
    a tip of her ear above the sheaves,
    nearly invisible to the eye, listening
    for your heartbeat.

Figure

HOW FEW BONES to a box.
    How small the box built
    of sticks and mucilage.
    How few songs sung.

    The human figure should not be
    viewed by itself. Even Brobdignags
    are very small without
    the trap of vestments,
    webs of jewellery and lies,
    the pink patina of strong blood.

    Alone on a bed, even the sheets
    look too big. They swath the limbs,
    wind the torso. Viewed from above,
    the human figure is too spare
    for reckoning. Too slight
    to tally, too thin to whistle, too odd
    to save more than a moment.

    The human figure is. It is very.
    By itself. It is smaller
    than thought. It is flesh
    without figure. It is
    human and very small.
    Our body. Our thought.

Missing

THESE SAME BEDS of red and purple
      flowers bleed across this perfect lawn,
      the stone tower blasted still, bleached
      as desert bone. Little changes.
      Petunias, a cartoonish ooze of vowels,
      a pig's name for the bright horns that
      rim this path I walk at noon, at three,
      at nine – playing out a long life
      in the sun or asleep beneath the snow.

To come full circle when some, arrested
at the top of their arc, broke their dive
into black water and did not surface for love
or argument, is to return on this path,
where blooms are tended each day, with
neither gravestone nor urn to talk to
about the hole in me where the wind
whistles through, where I know
exactly what I'm missing.

Dear Andy:

I AM NOT calling because
    the telephone betrays me daily
    with news from the afflicted world.
    My life is engraved by dying.
    I write to you and still hear their voices,
    hissing over wires across the wide country.
    I've come to hate the ringing – I burn
    a hard blue flame to melt the black snake's cord.

    Here, the texture of the morning sun isn't enough
    to light a slate noon sky. But at dawn,
    you are a muscled plume of smoke –
    always beyond the bounds of my hands or heart,
    you leap, quixotic, through hoops
    designed to distance.

    If someday you solidify into flesh and bone
    to stand bigger than life in my backyard,
    steam rising from your black hair,
    I will unplug the serpent, tear up my bill
    and dance the rhumba in red shoes.
    My arms will be your last hoop.

Memorial

HIP-DEEP IN backyard raspberry canes,
  I search for sweet
  flashes of red beneath
  spiky stems and broad leaves.
  Rare red nuggets ping one by one into my tin,
  treasure in this overgrown garden.

  Yesterday after his memorial
  we changed from our dresses into shorts
  and sat on the porch.
  You laughed at someone's joke,
  turned your head to the sun,
  and I saw the prize among your dark curls,
  a single long grey hair,
  no, two, a hard-won harvest
  while his last winter
  became just another spring,
  and I turned my head
  to the leafy apple tree
  that sprouts no fruit but
  the yellow balloons we tied in his memory.

In Sorrow's Kitchen

THERE'S A FRIDGE full of casseroles
    with notes taped to the lids
    — microwave five mins., call
    if you want to talk — more food
    than she could ever want, she could eat
    and eat and taste nothing, not
    sweet cakes nor succulent stews,
    she puts down the gold-edged plate
    and picks at the gilt

    at dawn, she beats the early light
    into batter for muffins, lemon loaves,
    cinnamon squares — shoves the pastries
    into the flustered hands of whoever
    rings the doorbell: friends, the postman,
    canvassers against disease

    she begs the lights off and sits
    with tea growing cold while night turns
    as dark as the inside of her head,
    until the sun's loud rise
    demands another day

    warily upright on the floor
    sorrow scrubbed clean, she misses
    what she never knew could leave
    because she never saw it arrive —
    sorrow feeds her until she
    throws its crumbs to the sparrows,
    always hungry

The Hiding Place

ALL WE REALLY want is
   to tunnel in each other
   from the hot storm of the world,
   shelter in the cave the heart makes when
   it folds in to a dark burrow,
   walls of red and deep umber

   but we will huddle almost anywhere,
   beneath broken glass or torn clothing,
   under wet leaves that cling to our faces
   when we skitter to another hole,
   another rotted place in the wall,
   behind the cupboard where no one
   would think of looking
   for someone small

   and in the hollowed heart, we plug
   the hole we made on impact
   with greeting cards and grocery bags,
   cotton and fibreglass, whatever
   keeps the cave from collapse, whatever
   guards against the moment when
   the cupboard is yanked from the wall
   by a hard hand
   and we are found
   even smaller
   than we thought

Mourning

DARK BIRTH,
      shouldering down
      a narrow canal, skull
      compressed by passage,
      the tunnel squeezing your head
      into a long torpedo, the pain
      unbearable, but in saying
      so you have borne it,
      you are born

      with an iceberg
      lodged behind your eye, jutting
      up into your brain, a numbing ache,
      a long blue anaesthetic, close enough
      to touch if you weren't so
      tired, if you wanted to
      open your eyes, if
      you wanted to
      want,
      if.

Grip

Sometimes I think I own him, sometimes
　　for weeks at a stretch I keep a life-grip
　　on the rippling arm of Death, I stake
　　my claim, I keep a clean house for so rough
　　a customer, I work against my will
　　to please, his sour breath on my cheek,
　　the fat worm of a scar on my neck.

　　I gave up
　　flesh and bone to hang
　　off his crooked arm. He scratches
　　my initials inside his elbow, I rub
　　the raw raised letters.

　　He takes others, women and men,
　　lovers or legion who cling to him
　　like dry leaves, upturned faces pale,
　　so close to his heat, waiting for answers
　　he never gives. On days when he loves another
　　for five minutes, or ten, or even a week,
　　I sleep, membraned in sooty sheets until
　　the morning he stands beside me at the stove,
　　runs his grimy hand up the ladder of my spine,
　　fingers the scar and says,
　　How've you been, I've missed you.

To My Milton Professor

Our torments may in length of time
Become our Elements
– *Paradise Lost*

THAT UNAVAILABLE WINTER sky
    and inside, the lake of fire – no wonder
    paradise was lost. I couldn't fathom Eden;
    so I footnoted someone else's thoughts
    on drowned youth, the agony of heroes.
    Who would not sing for Lycidas? I tuned up,
    a gifted parrot, unoriginal
    thought on original sin.

Years have crawled up my throat; I
buried Lycidas a dozen times. Still he
comes back, no matter what I sing,
a torso dripping elegaic mud,
a viscous ooze. A dirge
unwritten: no fresh woods,
no pastures new.

Instead I remember the last
of the men I called sir, the last
time I feared poetry –
no hard shove out of Heaven
but a scrawl in green ink, *Your analysis
is not brilliant, but will serve
if you avoid these leaps of imagination,*
and I tripped away, a mark on my
head full of rhyme.

Now he has crossed the river and
age waits for me in the stairwell,
it rachets my knees whenever I climb.
Most days what I know is small
enough to carry in my front pocket.
Torment or true element, I roam
the sorrowed earth, armed with nothing but
paper and a pair of poring eyes.

Breathing November

WHEN A RUSTING summer turns to lungfuls
    of frost and cold smoke, and wet streets
    eat through thin soles, then a frail man
    shivers beneath wool or down. He hangs on,
    neck and wrists corded as if clinging
    to a bone-cold November precipice,
    a dark drop, a long fall to spring,
    a plague of empty rooms that multiply,
    multiply. I hold my breath and refuse
    to write an elegy.

But one by one, kidney and spleen chill
and shut down, suspend his soul in a thinning
body as in a glacier. (We press against
the grey wall of ice, we see him,
a frozen specimen, so well-preserved,
say the scientists, so life-like,
say the mourners. We all turn into
scientists, don spectacles and
hypothesize cures. We only seem
smarter.)

March out like a lamb, on the church steps,
a silky breeze shocks us,
tugs at our wool mourning. The lover carries
ashes in a too-small urn. I know November
comes every year, and I listen
hard to love; the things of this world
beck and call. A glass of water,
a worn wooden floor, the cat curled
on my feet all night. All night. When I breathe
November, it does not last forever.

⋈ Part III

ONE KISS LEAVES YOU

Drought

GOING THIRSTY
    or unkissed
    gives you the same
    sand at the back of the throat

    you swallow
    and don't relieve the parched ache,
    it takes the mouth of a bottle
    or a lover to draw out
    the lake within you,
    your body 87% water in which
    63 cents of chemicals and salt
    float and form into cells
    that multiply and mutate,

but it takes water to prime the pump,
to draw water up
the curved well of your body
to your mouth, stretch the palate,
soften the lips, keep back
your smile because you can't
smile and drink, you can't smile
and kiss at the same time,

the way one never quenches,
the way one kiss leaves you thirsty,
the way one kiss leaves you

Love: Step-By-Step Instructions

BEGIN WITH WHAT is before you:
        a cat. A perfect square of blue.
    The luminous finish of a book.
        Evenly buttered toast.

Spend some time with your subject:
        watch carefully, everything changes.
    The cat will shed, the blue deepen to indigo
        or fade to mauve,

the prose will begin to irk you with
        its neatly tended plot,
the toast will cool, congeal, harden.
        Stay steady.

When you feel ready, switch your attention
        to human beings. (If you feel
thwarted by the toast, repeat.
        People are more sensitive than bread.)

Begin again with whoever sits before you,
        with whoever you find
right here. Don't plan it, don't try
        to trick your eye.

Love that person for one minute. Time it.
        Remember the backs of the ears,
imagine the occasional bad haircut.
        Remember fits of pique

and long silences. Remember others have loved
        them, for at least a minute, before you.
Let the attempt humble you, let it scrape
        against your organs like a pumice stone,

and love them anyway. When you have loved
        30 people a day for a year,
locate the Object of your Affection. (You'll
        find it to harder now to separate

dross from gold, but persevere.)
        Sit the person down and look.
If they ask why you are grinning,
        tell them the truth.

Tell them it takes eyes and mouth and hands
        and a supple wrist to love.
It takes three meals a day and a sheet
        of bus tickets. It demands detail,

and incredible gall. It takes
        the best part of you with no
guarantee. Practice is important.
        Pay close attention. Try this at home.

Reasons Why

YOU START WHEN I walk into the room, and I see that
some tics speak of love and distraction, some nerves run
on pure synaptic glory: it makes me make trouble, it
jumps me up like a car battery, my lost pulse found

a faint white scar runs into your upper lip, it keeps
secrets I can only guess at: you shaving with a shaky
hand, or in a drunken adolescent fight, or before your
wife's breakdown, when she slid from the kitchen with a
corkscrew and no bottle of wine, and you froze

there was never any question – if you start when I walk
into the room, if you jitter under my gaze, if your breath
hitches under my smile, there are reasons why love lives
in distraction

don't flinch until   you are sure of the pain

Pointing Out the Bluebird

PERCHED ON THE topmost
    branch of a young pine
    still, in the morning heat

    a slash of blue wings
    – you can't fool me –
    rises on singing cricket air

    tiny enough for a robin to bully
    or snack for the hawk
    cruising the valley,

    the bluebird knows
    no more about happiness
    than you or I

    newly returned to the path,
    grass still clinging
    to our backs

Moving In

I WORSHIP THE goddess of good glassware,
    pluck newspaper blossoms from vases,
    scrub crockery, rinse bone china.
    As the water darkens
    with printer's ink,
    words float
    to the slick surface,
    balloon, and
    drain away.

To fill the empty space is
less chore than creation:
a ruby crystal universe,
worlds glazed in blue bowls,
the ping of crystal
set in a high cupboard.

2.

There is no home but
what you make with
paint and whistles
at twilight, what
you stick together with
spit and splinters. Others
will squint at the sharp
angle of the roof, or say
it will be nice once you
fix it. You must care for
each bent nail, each cracked
tile, the frayed

edges of carpets
and bones left in boxes.

Oil hinges, welcome
a spider to spin her filmy web
high in the bedroom corner.
Pat the cat. Pad across and
across your new floor
in your bare feet.
Nothing matters but *hi I'm home,*
even if no one answers. Nothing
stops here but the whole
world.

Facts and Arguments

A DEER WANDERS up from the river bank, swift
    hooves on concrete. She runs safe for a block,
    but still at the corner of River and Osborne,
    she's struck by a car, her legs stiffened
    by the bray of neon. A block away,
    we unpack and re-wire the kitchen, split
    sprays of copper from casing. My ankle predicts
    rain and hard work. The park
    across the street looks less like Paris
    every day, leaves pale with cold. The sketcher,
    the man who scribbles scowls, sits hunched
    on the bench, and the pug that struts
    the path twice a day snorts at him,
    neighbourhood watch. It rains, old
    wounds are never wrong. I collect this place
    the way I collected you, facts and arguments.
    Novels say love ruins everything,
    and poetry. The cat has a window
    and eight naps a day, she's the same. We
    wake each morning dazed by the echo
    of old lovers who won't listen,
    who talk as if nothing has changed,
    as though our lives are a slip of the tongue,
    as though any gypsy could tell the story:
    how we wandered up from the river,
    sniffing the rough burn of rubber, swift
    grace and danger.

Phantom Limb

I.

MY UNCLE GOT his wooden leg in the war,
    used to knock on it like it was a small door
    that opened inwards, my uncle asking for
    permission to enter himself. He claimed
    the leg was hollow, and bet me a quarter
    he'd eat the most roast and Yorkshire pudding
    at dinner. My mother told me not to stare,
    but when he sank deep into a soft chair,
    an inch of dark polished wood showed
    between rolled pantcuff and sober black sock;
    a firm branch, a solid weapon if brandished,
    if swung. My uncle was a tall tree, a redwood
    hoisting himself from the easy chair, stumping
    down the hall to the dinner table. He never said
    whether he woke at night to a burning itch,
    the old leg calling him from the mud where
    he had left it and another boy who screamed
    for him and mother as the stretcher
    bore his body past a break in the trench.

II.

After the operation, all the adults insisted
she was fine, *adjusting so well to her
prosthesis,* that lisping antiseptic word,
a mash of prophylactic and hypothesis,
sex and theory, a guess about desire.
When I sat on the empty space on her bed,
she said *Get off my leg.* Her replacement limb
stood false sentry in the hospital closet,
leaning against her pea jacket
like a tipsy sailor's mate, the molded foot
already sporting her worn loafer, the left one,
an impostor at the ball, a fibreglass Cinderella.
She learned to walk on three legs: the steady
right, the chafing left, the wayward
old leg pulling her awry, begging
one more chance to take her places
the body refused, to find the way home.

Venom

Bees crawl and shiver in the apiary.
    The keeper, gloved and veiled
    as a member of a holy order,
    slides each drawer open to see
    bees clinging to flats of honeycombs,
    polishing each hexagon with pollened legs,
    dust from a sweet road. She reaches in, bees
    cover her arms and head, living velvet,
    a swarm of dark fuzz. She's been stung only
    ten times this season, a good average,
    enough to ward off chills.

    Her first sting at twelve years old, a hot
    nodule of pain shrugged off even as
    her shoulder throbbed, dismissed
    for the wry pleasure of being tough
    in front of girls queasy with second-hand panic
    and boys wary of a girl who would not weep
    at the glowing ache, red as a poked coal.
    But then still in the milling knot of children,
    now through the blanket of curious bees,
    she sees Bridget's stone-white face,
    her cousin dead at six from a sting
    that closed her throat and bruised her eyes;

a shadow who shames her arrogant good health
and belief in the invincible,
even with tragedy breathing in
great lungfuls of the day somewhere
out there, if not here,
the drawers of sweet venom
shut tight for today.

Home Birth

HER SECOND CHILD was induced by extra-spicy mu shu
vegetable and broccoli with black bean sauce, the slices
of red pepper and carrot coated with extra cayenne that
awoke the ticking alchemy of push and dive, and the boy
who slid from her body eighteen hours later polished
her to a roseate sheen, the boy who lay propped on the
long bones of her thighs, and then in my arms, that boy
who kicked and chirruped and fixed me with his grave
eyes, murmuring long strings of syllables in a language
he insisted I knew, a first speech about the alarm clock of
body, about the rush of water, about the air on his skin,
about being born on these blue sheets, his mewing so
much like my cat's arrival home after a four-day
walkabout, when she burst from the bushes, tail high,
hungry, tired from the trip but with more than enough
voice, as much voice as the boy, to say *let me tell you
where I've been I'm here I'm back let me tell you
everything.*

Horizon

I'M NOT OVER the swept threshold
    of my mother's house when she says
    come see what I've done with the garden.
    Threading through the cool dark rooms,
    I am a needle steadied for darning,
    the fuss-and-fix-it that made me,
    that chafed me. But by the back door,
    on that single step that passes as a porch,
    I stop, rooted because

    my mother has finally done it.
    She's gardened the surface of the earth entire,
    hoed and watered the world into neat rows,
    tinkered the planet into good working order.
    She's planted all the way to the horizon,
    its calm line drawn perpendicular to
    sixty staked rows of stringbeans,
    pulling the sun down each night,
    yanking it up each morning. Raspberry canes
    swarm the middle distance, snarling
    their fruit forward. Rhubarb begs
    for pies, heliotrope dogs the sun,
    the spider-spread of portulaca
    webs the soil at my toes.

My mother walks the rows,
bends to turn a tomato and show
me the blush, how the sun ripens
one side first.

Take This

THIS IS THE ground. bend to touch it. here ants carry eight times their own weight, the price of eating. this is wood, this splintered log, this burnable rock. this is how to swing an axe. plant your feet wide. wear boots. keep your toes attached.

this is the garden, its riot of green. the curled leaves of potatoes. the grasping pumpkin vines. mind your ankles. this is how to harvest. crouch, dig, pull, hands brown with soil. no gloves, ever. the dirt inverts your handprint on the sink. the refrigerator. the back of a neck.

this is the arch of sky, the shoving clouds. this is how to survive the wind. find shelter. stand beneath it and call. the wind wrenches your voice into tumbleweed, a blown web, a torn feather.

this is paper, a stripped heart of tree you hold in your hand, a tawny whiff of ink. it says nothing you don't already know. this paper says nothing. knows everything. gives it all away.

this is a gift, the last you will receive. this is how to take it. stretch out one arm. uncurl your fingers. hold it. hold it.

Part IV

A Half-Sea House

Water Damage

THERE'S A STORY of
    a not-so-little mermaid
    who tells the sea witch no,
    she will not give up her voice
    for shapely smooth
    legs and a landed lover;
    a mermaid who halloos
    her shore-bound man from the waves,
    "Hey! It's me! I still love you,
    even though I'm half-fish!
    Love me, love my fin."
    And he does.

They live together in a half-sea house
with the tile floor flooded two feet deep;
she swims and sings, he wears hip waders
and doesn't use the toaster.
Dust is never a problem,
though water damage is,
but they just laugh
and caulk the windows.

At night,
when he snores in his wetsuit
and she floats on her back,
she shivers and thinks
of eternal silence,
of sharp knives beneath the feet
she'll never have.

There's a statue in Copenhagen,
our mermaid not pining out to sea,
but curled on land, her children
clustered around her tail,
mouth open in a whoop,
her caulking gun in hand.

Diana in the Autumn Wind

SHE WORE A t-shirt that read
　　warning: will fight back, she took
　　exception to badly sliced bagels
　　and a shared phone, she treaded water
　　and told stories of sexual escapade
　　while she kicked her chlorined toes, she
　　walked to the bus in the hawk and spit of
　　that limp summer, humidity
　　killing her curls

　　she wore a long dress to soft
　　ball games and jeans to board meetings,
　　strapped her bow across her back, filled
　　her quiver with dried apricots (claimed
　　a delicate stomach, only trusted
　　what she bought herself)

　　last fall, she released the guillemot
　　nested hungry in the cliff of her breast,
　　but kept it on a ten-foot tether, tugged it
　　back, reeled it in like a fighting fish,
　　until the wings buffeted
　　her, rising from the earth in a blur,
　　wind and cloth and sinew,
　　a beaked woman, a legged kite

The Rapture of Miss Crawford

THE WINKING OF the scarlet scarab
  pin behind the glass
  reminds me of Eileen

  by Cheops' Grand Pyramid, in Red Square,
  on the banks of Mother Ganges,
  clutching pocketbook, squinting in the sun,

  buying brooches, bracelets,
  necklaces, rings, scatter pins,
  earrings and crucifixes,

  packing them home to Edinburgh,
  to her dank Oxgangs flat, cataloguing each piece
  by colour, soft metal and precious stone

  guarded by jackal-headed Anubis:
  oh Eileen, dead in your tweeds these three years,
  gone to join Osiris in the Beautiful West

  after half a century of travel,
  your pirate's booty gleams
  from a polished private case

  in a corner of the National Museum of Scotland:
  a well-kept will, a last testament
  to reveal to the world

  a retired typist from Oxgangs was not
  entombed in a herringbone suit and sensible shoes
  but lives, a scarab scarlet in the eye of Ra

Europa

Don't think for a minute
    the girl astride the bull's back is
    any kind of victim. She refuses to
    grip his neck with her knees, will not
    pinch that thick corrugated muscle
    with her thighs, though she teeters atop
    his ridged spine, the ark on Ararat.
    This girl is hard iron naked,
    legs spread and bent for stirrups
    that aren't there, the way a woman
    opens herself to tests, to birth,
    to speed. She balances on the brahma hump,
    her coccyx sharp as a sting;
    she's a trick rider without
    benefit of buckskin or boot.
His hooded eyes almost coy, he snorts
and bends, obedient as waves or wind.
She reaches for the ring in his nose
to steer, but he snakes out his tongue,
wraps it around her wrist like an eel.
Her eyes grow heavy as flint, dark as
her ache to ride, to raise dust,
to return to rock. She can't keep
her eyes open; she thumps her heels
against his wide ribcage, and turns him
into the sun. She curls on
the broad bed of his back, and he walks
north-west, hooves slicing the dust,
careful of his cargo, the burdened girl
and her beast.

Shakespeare's Sister

The force of her own gift alone drove her to it . . .
who shall measure the heat and violence of the poet's
heart when caught and tangled in a woman's body?
– Virginia Woolf, *A Room of One's Own*

My brother was a talented man. 38 plays, 154 sonnets,
4 long narrative poems and a threnody on the death of
chaste lovers, all with a little Latin and less Greek – well.
A genius in his own time, surely.

But his appetite burned a hole in our family's pockets, he
wouldn't sew gloves, wouldn't apprentice to the new
bailiff, just scribbled, then was gone to London. We
weren't foolish – there was nowhere else for him, and
nothing for it but to follow.

Will made enough in London to carouse, but sent no
coin home. Our father snored beneath the alehouse
table, too drunk to oppose what Ann and I concocted by
the fire one cold night, the children hungry in their
beds. I, being more than common tall, attired myself on
all points as a man and set out. I crossed Clopton Bridge
on a cold St. George's Day, my brother's 25th feast-day. I
found him face down, feasting on a puddle of his own
spew, nothing new in that.

No longer a woman, I didn't clean and coddle him, but
booted his backside like the dog he was and swore on
his children's eyes that he'd send money home if I had to
sell his body as a rent boy. I locked him in his shabby
rooms, kept the key in my fist, and he wrote three plays
a year. Some were good. People started to notice. An Earl

commissioned some sonnets, offered gold for my dark hair sketched into my brother's verse. Money was money. My namesake niece in Stratford grew tall enough to preen and call herself Judith.

My brother was a talented man. But for me, who never again wore a dress, who played manager for twenty years, his greatest feat lay in how he turned our family fortunes, our green and yellow melancholy, into the great Globe itself. A person, to write, needs a room of one's own. A door that locks. Someone to hold the key.

Wendy

WHEN I SAID I wanted to be a mother, I meant like my mother, with Nana to look after the children, and me coming in to kiss them good-night in my long white gloves on my way out to the opera, smelling of perfume and face powder, trailing a tuxedoed and moustached husband to smile and hold doors for me.

There were so many of them, though, who needed a mother, that I said yes at first. So many lost boys, so many dirty faces, I thought if I could just clean behind their ears a bit they would transform into the kind of boys my brothers had been, bookish John, sweet Michael. But these boys were different – they shot pool and smoked crack and some of them sold their bodies for money every night and I couldn't be enough mother for them no matter how good I was and they stared at me though pinhole eyes and said *mothermother are you my fuckin' mother* until I couldn't take any more and came home. I joined the order shortly after – no little boys here, no men at all except for the occasional visiting Brother, so cool and clean they're more like cats or women.

I'm in charge of scrubbing the abbey floors. My mother died years ago, but I keep her opera gloves in the drawer of my bedside table. Once a month, I unwrap them from their blue tissue paper and inhale their scent. It's enough.

Eurydice

FOLLOWING YOU SEEMED
    like a good idea at the time:

    Hades was no Vegas,
    and Pluto was an old-man bore –
    chock full of conspiracy theories,
    all *evil plan* this, *hidden agenda* that.
    When I told him the best revenge
    was living well, he thought I said,
    living hell and cackled
    This is the place!
    Who do you think aimed
    the viper at your ankle?
    Musicians get all the good women.
    Spittle ran down his chin
    and he stank of brimstone and beer
    like you'd expect, only
    worse. I was glad to hear you
    playing the lyre, coming
    down to me.

But walking out
single file in the dark,
your words floated back to me,
the house you would build,
the children I would bear, and I saw
myself pounding linens white on the rocks,
ignored by the river gods, my hands red
year round, the house smelling of scorched
mutton and your swiped palmprints
reaching from their clay walls to close
me in their cold dust.
I slowed. I stopped.
In the pale light, I saw
the back of your neck stiffen, then
you looked back.

I said good-bye but meant
there was nothing you could have done.

Nymph of the Fountain

ALWAYS HUNGRY AND always cold,
    I never felt the water
    streaming from my hair, soaking
    the chairs I sat on, pooling in the bed,
    filling my shoes like swamped boats.
    I turned the air humid. I fogged my lover's windows,
    obscured his precious view of charwomen
    leaving for work, of broken chimney-pots.
    He frowned and rubbed a spot
    clear with his cuff, then
    had to change his shirt.

    A grinding rattle of water caught in
    my ear, my inland sea. My fingers pruned.
    A fine cool mist arced from my mouth.
    I was Lot's other wife, the pillar of water,
    the woman who did not look back,
    the woman who would not meet her husband's eyes,
    who feared desert exile
    because there was no way to drown.

Growing Feathers

... the owl was a baker's daughter.
– *Hamlet* 4.5.43

NO, THE OWL was a banker's daughter

    not a plump girl with flour to her elbows
    and breasts like soft loaves of bread
    but a watchful girl with
    glasses, all angled elbows and
    accrued interest, not
    a crude interest,
    whose father never worried
    about her losing her head,
    it was screwed on so
    tight

    once, the banker's daughter met
    the farmer's daughter
    coming home from market:
    "there's this handsome travelling salesman
    without nowhere to stay tonight –
    if Father lets him sleep in the barn,
    I'll leave my window open ..."

    the banker's daughter hooted
    her derision
    and went home to feather her nest

she didn't need to be pretty,
she had savvy
and gold bonds in her bedroom safe

but he was handsome, smart and
(what a catch!) thrifty —
relieved at last to share the weight
of being so damned careful,
that night she slept
folded into him like a wing,
hand curled around the safe key
she gave him as a lover's locket,
and smiled in her favourite dream —
loose in a bank vault,
swimming in cold hard cash

she woke alone,
the key flung atop the empty safe,
his pillow skinned of its case,
her money slung over his back,
careful savings
gone for tankards of ale
and shoes for another woman's brats

her eyes bulged,
thin arms spanned wide
and big feet curved talons
around a branch
while her mouth's sharp line
rounded only to muse,
who would woo her?
who?

now the key never leaves her grasp
and she sees so much better
in the dark

Origin of Species

CONSIDER THE ONLY evidence: a few feet of film
    shot with a shaky camera, the beast strolling,
    casual as a sailor just put to port,

    that long rolling stride, sea-grace odd on a creature
    of size. Consider the smell, dank and musky
    as boot insoles over a hot air vent.

    Consider the sound, a marshland suck and squish,
    a deep boreal silence sighing away
    two blocks from your house.

    The dark walking bulk swallows any hue,
    even when the streetlight in the back lane
    turns everything else a hepatic yellow,

    the creature stops by your gate, then ambles
    over your manicured lawn, unimpressed
    by the submissive grass. It forces

    the window frame with its shadow,
    shoves in a shower of wood and glass.
    No time now to consider

    the creature's arms as they reach,
    a savage hug and stagger, your face against
    the hot fur. No time to think about where

it takes you, or how no one believes or knows
where to look. No one hears your breath hitch,
or sees your eyes darken. You thicken,
grow taller, sprout matted hair – you become the brute,
the link to the green world. The creature mulches
into leaves and broken twigs, a deadfall,

a vanished grave, and you lurk alone beneath
the calling trees. You gouge bark in ragged strips,
and when you hear the camera's whir,

look over your dark shoulder, see only an insectile eye
and cloth-stick legs, and turn away
into the trees. We can't prove a thing.

Troll Lessons

LESSON 1:

    Stop shaving your legs.
    If the hair grows in darker,
    coarser, so much the better.
    Ditto armpits.

    Throw the tweezers away.
    Attempt to grow your eyebrows
    into the centre of your forehead.
    Not everyone can be a troll.
    It's damp under those bridges –
    you need all the hair you can sprout.

    Toothpaste, deodorant, moisturizer –
    toss them all. Look in the mirror.
    If you are speechless at the sight –
    good. If you lift your lip to admire
    your canines – you're ready.

    (If you laugh or dig
    through the trash for your tweezers,
    you are not ready to troll yet.
    Turn away and gnaw off all
    your fingernails. Start from
    scratch.)

Lesson 2:

 Find a bridge over a dry river
 gorge or blasted valley.
 Stone is best, although
 some trolls like the way
 the wind creaks wooden struts
 on stormy nights.

 What you want is a good brace for
 your broad feet when you hear
 clip, clop, clip overhead.
 What you want is a solid echo
 for your howl.

 You want Lilith's corded neck,
 Kali's double row of teeth, their
 long muscled arms. You want the clatter
 of hooves striking granite.

Lesson 3:

 Afterwards, pick your teeth
 with the thinnest of bones.
 Everything has its uses.

 Contrary to what you may have heard,
 trolls are not unhygienic.
 Our mouths are probably cleaner
 than yours. Kiss me.

Classic Beauty

WHEN PERSEUS SNUCK up on Medusa,
    sandals not as stealthy as he thought,
    her snakes woke first and
    flicked warning tongues in her ear;
    a quick glance over her shoulder
    petrified him in mid-step.

    He revived the next morning
    after she was long gone, and said,
    "Man, last night I was so stoned . . ."

    Finding a skull-white boulder,
    he flung on a heap of seaweed,
    held it aloft and shouted,
    "I have slain the beast!
    Look on me, Atlas,
    and quaver!"

    On another continent,
    wrinkles slither onto Medusa's face –
    world's oldest surviving Gorgon.
    She invests well, retires early.

She combs her green curls back,
moves to the coast,
opens a bookstore,
sells copies of *The Beauty Myth*
and keeps a section on reptiles
by the cash register for impulse buys.

A sign on her shop door reads,
Here lives the beast.
Look on me, world
and discover.

Notes

Many of these poems owe a debt to other literary works or visual art:

"South of Discovery" was written after reading Rudy Wiebe's *A Discovery of Strangers*.

"Figure" was a response to a line in Carol Shields' *Thirteen Hands*: "It's a fact that the human figure, seen on its own, is very small."

"In Sorrow's Kitchen" takes its title from Susan Straight's novel *I Been in Sorrow's Kitchen and I Licked Out All the Pots*.

"Breathing November" owes a debt to Margaret Atwood's "Man in a Glacier."

"Nymph of the Fountain" comes from Virginia Woolf's *The Waves*.

"Diana in the Autumn Wind" and "Mourning" take their titles from paintings by Paul Klee.

"Europa" is titled after Leo Mol's sculpture of the same name.

"The Rapture of Miss Crawford" commemorates Eileen Crawford and her 300-piece jewellery collection, installed in the National Museum of Scotland in the summer of 1994.

"Shakespeare's Sister" quotes liberally from *As You Like It, Twelfth Night,* and *The Tempest*.

Acknowledgements

Thank you to my editor, Allan Briesmaster, for his sharp
eye and gracious manner, and for all his work in promoting
new poets.

These poems owe their space on the page to the many people
who read them thoughtfully in the early stages: Susan
Ioannou, Betsy Struthers, Helen Humphreys, Ruth Roach
Pierson, Maureen Hynes, Alison Hancock, Marion O'Rourke,
Laura McLachlan, Robert Priest, Miranda Pearson, Di Brandt,
Kirsten Romaine Jones, Ryan Land, and Sharanpal Ruprai.
Special thanks to the Sage Hill Writing Experience for the
time to write and space to think.

"Follow" is for Peter Leslie. "Home Birth" is for Tamara
Elliott. "Horizon" is for Kay Stone. "Facts and Arguments"
is for John Roscoe.

Some of these poems first appeared in *Prairie Fire,*
Contemporary Verse 2, Grain, Dandelion, Other Voices,
Pottersfield Portfolio, The Fiddlehead, McGill Street,
and *Room of One's Own,* and in the anthologies *Doors of
the Morning* and *Waiting For You To Speak* (both from
Unfinished Monument Press), *The Edges of Time* (Seraphim
Editions), and the forthcoming *Madwoman in the Academy.*

Some of these poems also appeared in my two chapbooks,
This Speaking Plant (Unfinished Monument Press, 1997) and
Breathing November (Staccato Press, 1999).

"Holding Ground" won second prize in *Dandelion's* 1994
poetry contest. "Pointing Out the Bluebird" won third prize in
Pottersfield Portfolio's 1996 short poem contest. "The Onion
Eater" won third prize in *Prairie Fire's* 1997 poetry contest.

TANIS MACDONALD lives in Winnipeg and Victoria, after spending a number of years working in the Toronto HIV and mental health communities. Her poetry and prose have appeared in journals across Canada, and her first chapbook, *This Speaking Plant,* won the Acorn-Rukeyser Award in 1996. She is currently a graduate student specializing in Canadian poetry and poetics. This is her first full-length collection.